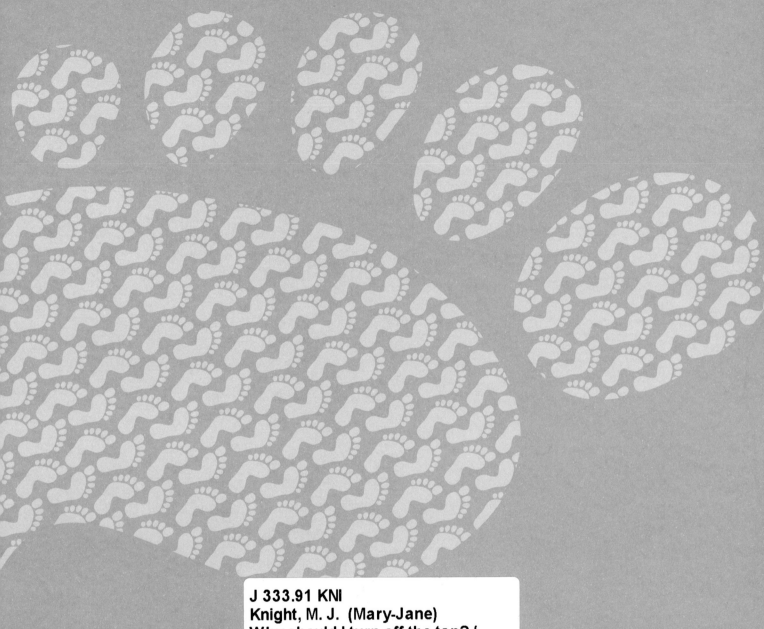

one small step

Why Should I
Turn Off the Tap?

M J Knight

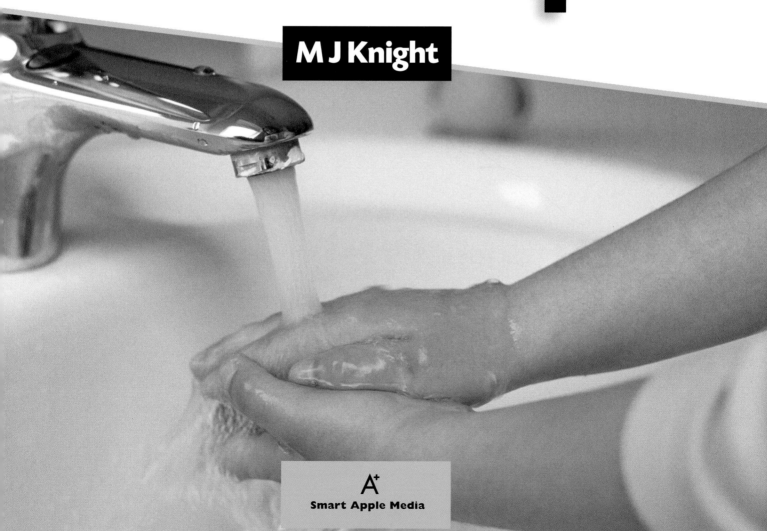

A+
Smart Apple Media

Smart Apple Media is published by Black Rabbit Books
P.O. Box 3263, Mankato, Minnesota 56002

Printed in China

Library of Congress Cataloging-in-Publication Data

Knight, M. J. (Mary-Jane)
    Why should I turn off the tap? / M.J. Knight.
    p. cm. — (Smart Apple Media. One small step)
    Summary: "Facts about why saving water is important and practical tips for kids about how they can contribute to water conservation"—Provided by publisher.
    Includes index.
    ISBN 978-1-59920-264-8 (hardcover)
    1. Water conservation—Juvenile literature. 2. Water—Waste—Juvenile literature. I. Title.
TD495.K585 2008
333.91'16--dc22

                                                                2008011377

Designed by Guy Callaby
Edited by Jinny Johnson
Illustrations by Hel James
Picture research by Su Alexander

Picture acknowledgements
Title page: Heide Benser/Zefa/Corbis; 4 Tom Van Sant, Geosphere Project/Planetary Visions/Science Photo Library; 7 Kit Houghton/Corbis; 8 Lars Langemeier/A.B./Zefa/Corbis; 9 Dennis M. Sabangan/epa/Corbis; 10 Momatiuk Eastcott/Corbis; 12 Tony Watson/Alamy; 13 Heide Benser/Zefa/Corbis; 14 Lester Lefkowitz/Corbis; 16 Frans Lemmens/Zefa/Corbis; 19 Edward Bock/Corbis; 20 Christopher Thomas/Getty Images; 23 Leslie Garland Picture Library/Alamy; 24 Mark Bolton/Corbis; 25 Tom Stewart/Corbis; 26 Ralf-Finn Hestoft/Corbis; 27 Martin Jones/Corbis; 28 Gideon Mendel/Corbis; 29 Howard Davies/Corbis.
Front cover: Danwer Productions/Alamy.

9 8 7 6 5 4 3 2 1

Contents

A Watery World

Earth is often called the blue planet because it looks blue from space. That's because water covers about three-quarters of the surface.

Nearly all the Earth's water is in the oceans, which means that it is salty. We can't drink this water or use it to grow food. Most of the freshwater on Earth is frozen solid in ice sheets at the North and South Poles. The tiny amount of freshwater that's not frozen is in streams, rivers, and lakes, or falls as rain.

In this view of the Earth, you can see how much of our planet is taken up by the Pacific Ocean.

Why Do We Need to Save Water?

Every year, there are more and more people living on Earth. But the amount of water stays the same. Everyone needs water to survive, so we must use it carefully to make sure there is enough to go around.

When you want a drink of water, you turn on a tap and there it is. But sometimes we all waste water or use more than we need. Always think about how much water you use and try not to waste it.

A Step in the Right Direction

You might think that what you do doesn't matter, but it matters very much. Every time you think about how much water you use, you are making a difference. Everyone can make a difference, and remember–every drop of water counts!

One Small Fact

If you could put all the world's water into a bucket, only one teaspoonful would be drinkable.

Water All Around

**Water is in the air and in the clouds.
It is in ice, rain, snow, sleet, and hail.**

There's water underground, as well as in ponds, streams, rivers, and lakes. Most of all, there's water in the oceans and seas. The way water moves around is called the water cycle. Rain, snow, and clouds are all part of this water cycle. There would be no life on Earth without water, so it is very precious.

The sun warms the water in oceans, rivers, and lakes.

Trees and plants also lose some water into the air as water vapor.

Some of the water turns into water vapor and rises into the air. This is called evaporation.

One Small Fact
In some places, rainwater soaks into the ground and trickles through tiny holes in rocks to make an underground pool called an aquifer.

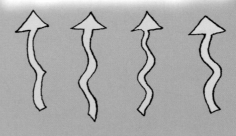

We drink water, wash with it, cook with it, and use it to grow crops and raise farm animals. The horses on the right are drinking at a water trough. We also use lots of water for making things.

Water vapor rises up into the atmosphere. Here it cools and turns into clouds. This is called condensation.

In very cold weather or at the tops of mountains, rain may fall as snow.

Rain falls from the clouds onto the Earth. Rainwater runs off the ground into streams, rivers, lakes, and oceans.

Some rainwater collects underground.

Problems with Water

There is more than enough water in the world for everyone. But there are some problems with water around the world.

Water can become dirty or polluted. At home, we mix water with dish soap to clean our dishes. In the countryside, farmers put fertilizers in water to help their crops grow. Factories mix water with metals and chemicals when they make things. All these things pollute water, and it has to be cleaned before it can be used again.

Lots of water is used when tin is taken from under the ground at this mine.

Cutting down trees also causes problems. People cut down trees to make fields, or to build houses, factories, and roads. But when rain falls on places where there are no trees, it doesn't seep into the ground to form springs and streams for us to take water from. It rushes away over the ground, and sometimes it causes floods.

A family stranded by floods waits to be rescued from the roof of their house in the Philippines.

Water on the Move

We move water around a lot, usually in pipes. This helps us use it to make things, such as cars, computers, or processed food.

In some parts of the world, water is taken away from where people live, leaving them with very little to use. The problem is worse in some countries than others. In North America, we have a good supply of water, but we still can't afford to waste it.

One Small Fact

In some countries in Africa, only half the people have a clean supply of water.

In the United States, the Colorado River doesn't flow as far as the ocean anymore, because people have taken so much water out of it.

How Much Water?

Making things and producing food uses lots of water. Here's how much water it takes to make some everyday items.

One Small Fact
The amount of water we use to make something is called embedded water.

cotton T-shirt 1,060 gallons (4,000 L)

apple 18 gallons (70 L)

glass of orange juice 45 gallons (170 L)

slice of bread 11 gallons (40 L)

sheet of paper 3 gallons (10 L)

glass of milk 53 gallons (200 L)

pair of leather shoes 2,100 gallons (8,000 L)

bag of chips 50 gallons (185 L)

burger 630 gallons (2,400 L)

Growing 2 pounds (1 kg) of potatoes takes 264 gallons (1,000 L) of water, but growing 2 pounds (1 kg) of beef takes 16 times as much.

car 105,700 gallons (400,000 L)

Where Does Tap Water Come From?

When you turn on a tap, water comes out of it. This water comes from holes in the ground called boreholes, from rivers, or from special lakes called reservoirs.

A water company makes sure that the water is clean. Then it pumps the water through pipes called water mains to our homes. Pipes inside our homes carry the water to taps over sinks and bathtubs and to toilets.

This water pipe carries water from a nearby river to a reservoir.

One Small Fact

A person can live for several weeks without eating, but only a few days without water.

Although there is more than enough freshwater on Earth for everyone, not everyone can turn on a tap to get water. In some parts of the world, people have to walk a long way for water every day. When they find it, the water may not be good to drink.

How Much Water Do We Use?

Most Europeans use 53 gallons (200 L) of water every day.

North Americans use twice as much water— 106 gallons (400 L) every day.

People in poorer parts of the world use much less water —just 3 gallons (10 L) of water every day.

Where Does Water Go?

When you pull out the plug in a sink, the water runs down waste pipes and into a drain.

From the drain, it runs into a bigger pipe called a sewer. Water and waste from showers, baths, and toilets goes into the sewers too. So does rainwater, which runs off the ground.

Wastewater is cleaned in tanks at a sewage treatment plant before it is pumped back into rivers.

The wastewater ends up in a place called a sewage treatment plant. Here it is cleaned in tanks. First the water is pumped through filters, which work like sieves and catch lumps, garbage, and grit. Then the water goes into another tank. Here solids sink to the bottom to form a sludge.

The sludge can be cleaned by blowing air into it, or by adding tiny living things called bacteria, which feed off the waste. When the water is clean again, the water company pumps it back into a river.

One Small Fact

Sewer pipes are usually made of concrete and can be big enough to walk through.

I Can Make a Difference

If people put garbage down the toilet, it causes problems at the sewage plant. So don't ever put garbage down the toilet. Toilets are meant to flush away the waste from our bodies and nothing else, except toilet paper.

Water to Drink

There is lots of water in our bodies and we all need to drink several glasses of water a day to stay healthy.

All drinks, including soda pop, contain some water. But the best liquid for your body is just water—with nothing added.

The water you drink helps your kidneys work better. Kidneys keep your blood clean and remove waste from your body. You get rid of the waste in your urine.

16

One Small Fact

Water helps you concentrate and do better at sports, so drink plenty.

I Can Make a Difference

When you want a drink of water, do you turn on the cold tap and wait for the water to run until it's cold? This wastes water. Instead, put a bottle of tap water in the fridge so you can have cold water any time you like without wasting a single drop.

Full of Water

Our bodies are full of water. The younger you are the more watery you are! Your brain is about three-quarters water. Your blood has even more water in it. Even your bones are one-fifth water!

Water at Home

Think about all the ways you use water in the kitchen.

Do you help with washing the dishes? Or perhaps your family has a dishwasher? If you rinse dishes under a running tap, lots of water runs down the drain and is wasted. It's much better to rinse them in a sink of water.

One Small Fact

You can save 24,000 gallons (92,000 L) of water a year by not letting the tap run. That amount could fill a whole swimming pool!

When you help with the dishes, remember to rinse plates and dishes in a sink of water, rather than under a running tap.

18

Do you ever make a cup of tea for your mom or dad? How much water do you put in the kettle? If you just put enough for the number of cups of tea you need, you will not only save water, you will save energy too.

If your family has a dishwasher, make sure the machine is full before you turn it on. A machine that's half full uses more than half the water to wash the dishes. A dishwasher can use between 9 and 12 gallons (34 and 45 L) of water for every load. Help your mom or dad check that it is full before it's turned on.

Water for Washing

The bathroom is where we use the most water. So what can you do to use less?

We need to wash every day—there's no escaping that! If your bathroom has a shower, you can use less water by taking a shower rather than a bath. Most baths use three times as much water as a shower.

One Small Fact

Not all showers use less water. A power shower uses more water in five minutes than it takes to fill a bath.

You can help save water by taking a short shower rather than a long, deep bath.

Can you find any dripping faucets in your house? If so, tell your mom and dad so they can get them fixed. That will save water too.

I Can Make a Difference

Turn off the tap when you brush your teeth. If you leave the tap running, you waste lots of water. Instead, fill up a plastic cup with water before you start. Use this to rinse your mouth and your toothbrush when you have finished brushing.

Flushed Away

What uses the most water in your house? Yes, it's the toilet. Every time we flush the toilet, gallons of water go down the drain along with the waste.

Everyone uses 13 gallons (50 L) of water a day just by flushing the toilet. Today, new toilets use less water than the older ones do. If your house has a toilet that is more than 14 years old, your family can save water by putting a brick in the toilet tank.

A family of four can use two bathtubs full of water every day just flushing the toilet.

One Small Fact

One toilet flush can use as much as 2.3 gallons (9 L) of water.

Your family could also get a device to put inside the toilet tank so it uses less water. There are several different types and you can find out about them from the company that supplies your water. These devices can save between one-quarter and three-quarter gallons (1 and 3 L) of water every time the toilet is flushed.

I Can Make a Difference

Putting a water-saving device inside your toilet tank can save 2,000 gallons (7,570 L) of water a year—enough for 100 baths!

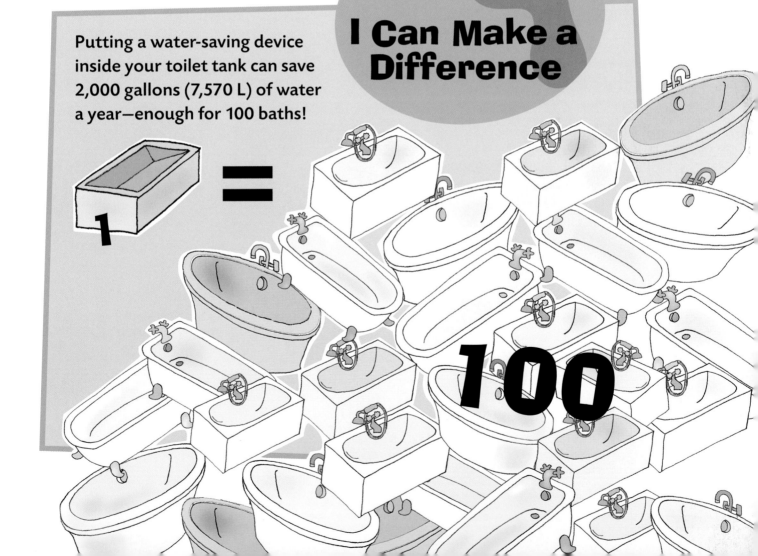

1 = 100

Using Water in the Garden

If you have a garden, there are lots of ways you can help to use less water there.

Do you ever help water the garden? If so, you can try to use less water when you do this. Perhaps you can persuade your family to buy a rain barrel. This stands in a corner of the yard and is connected to the drainpipes, so the rain that falls on the house runs into the barrel. Then you'll have lots of water for the plants.

If you collect rainwater in a rain barrel, you'll never have to turn on the tap to fill the watering can.

One Small Fact

If you water plants in the morning or evening, you need less water than if you water them in the middle of the day, when it is hotter.

I Can Make a Difference

Hoses use lots and lots of water, and sprinklers can use 132 gallons (500 L) of water an hour, so it's best to avoid these. Instead, you can offer to water the plants by filling up a watering can, either from a tap or from a rain barrel if you have one.

Something else that could make a difference is to find out about plants that need less water to grow. Could you plant some in your yard? If you have a big yard, you could plant trees and shrubs that will give some shade. That means the grass will not dry out as much when the sun shines.

Even a small tree can help make your yard cooler in hot and sunny weather.

Saving Water at School

Do you know how much water is used at your school? Do a water survey to find out how much water the school uses. Can you find ways to use less water at school?

Make a list of places where there are faucets and check them carefully to see whether any of them drip. Does everyone remember to turn off the faucet after they have washed their hands? If you find taps left running, you could talk to your teacher about whether the school might have push taps put in. These switch off automatically, so no one can accidentally leave the faucet running.

You can save water when washing your hands by always putting the plug in the sink before you turn on the tap.

I Can Make a Difference

Make a poster to put up, asking everyone to put the plug in the sink when they wash their hands, instead of washing them under running water. You could also make one to remind people to turn off the faucet when they have finished washing their hands.

SAVE WATER

REMEMBER!
Put in the plug when you wash your hands.

HAVE YOU TURNED OFF THE TAP?

If you have a school garden, find out if the school has any rain barrels for rainwater. If not, perhaps you could help raise some funds to buy one.

One Small Fact

Enough rain falls on the roofs of most elementary schools to fill nearly 19,000 rain barrels.

Watering cans use a lot less water than a hose.

Not Enough Water

Something else you can do at school is to find out about children and water in other countries.

About one in six of all the people in the world do not have any clean water. Nearly half the people who don't have clean water live in Africa. In some African countries, many families spend a long time every day walking to fetch water, which might be several miles away. Some children can't go to school because it is their job to fetch water for their families for drinking and cooking.

Think about all the times you use water during the day. Imagine what it would be like if you had to fetch water every time you needed it. You wouldn't have much time for anything else!

Many children in Zimbabwe in Africa spend a lot of time fetching and carrying water for their families.

There are several charities that raise money for projects that help people get clean water by digging wells or laying pipes. Use your school computers to find out about them. Perhaps you could choose a water charity for your school or class to support. Then you could organize some fund-raising activities to help children like you enjoy clean water as you do.

One Small Fact

Two-thirds of people live in areas of the world that have only a quarter of the world's rain.

Children in a village in Tanzania are thrilled with the clean water gushing from their pump.

Glossary

atmosphere
The atmosphere is a thick layer of gases that surrounds the Earth.

bacteria
Bacteria are tiny living things that are everywhere—in air, water, soil, animals, people, and food. They are so small that a million would fit on a pinhead.

borehole
A hole dug in the ground to reach water underground.

fertilizer
Chemicals put on the ground by farmers to help their crops grow. Natural fertilizers such as animal dung also help crops grow.

kidneys
You have two kidneys in your body, which help clean your blood. Urine is made in the kidneys.

reservoir
A large lake which supplies water to people.

sewage/sewage treatment plant
Sewage is human waste and wastewater, which runs into sewer pipes. Sewage ends up at a sewage treatment plant, where it is cleaned and pumped back into a river.

sewer
A large pipe that carries sewage. Sewers also carry rainwater that runs off the ground.

sleet
Rain that has some ice in it.

springs
Places where water wells up from underground.

water vapor
Water in the form of a gas in the air.

Web Sites

http://www.epa.gov/water/kids.html
Projects, art, and experiments to involve kids and students with environmental protection, from the Environmental Protection Agency (EPA).

http://ga.water.usgs.gov/edu/
Offers information on many aspects of water, along with pictures, data, maps, and an interactive center where you can give opinions and test your water knowledge.

http://www.ecokids.ca/pub/eco_info/topics/water/water/index.cfm
An interactive game shows players how to save water around the house.

http://www.wateraid.org/international/learn_zone/
The Web site of the charity WaterAid has lots of information and facts about water use. There is also a section on fund-raising for children under 11.
 Just a Drop charity Web site has information on its water-based projects.

http://www.tampagov.net/dept_Water/information_resources/Kids/
The city of Tampa, Florida provides water conservation tips for kids both inside and outside, plus games and a calendar.

http://www.olliesworld.com/planet/index.htm
A Web site that aims to help children think about taking care of the planet.

Index